To: Carolyn and John
grandparents of
Amelia Jane Neiman

may she "grow in wisdom
and stature, and in
favor with God and men."
    from the Adams
        July 7, 2003

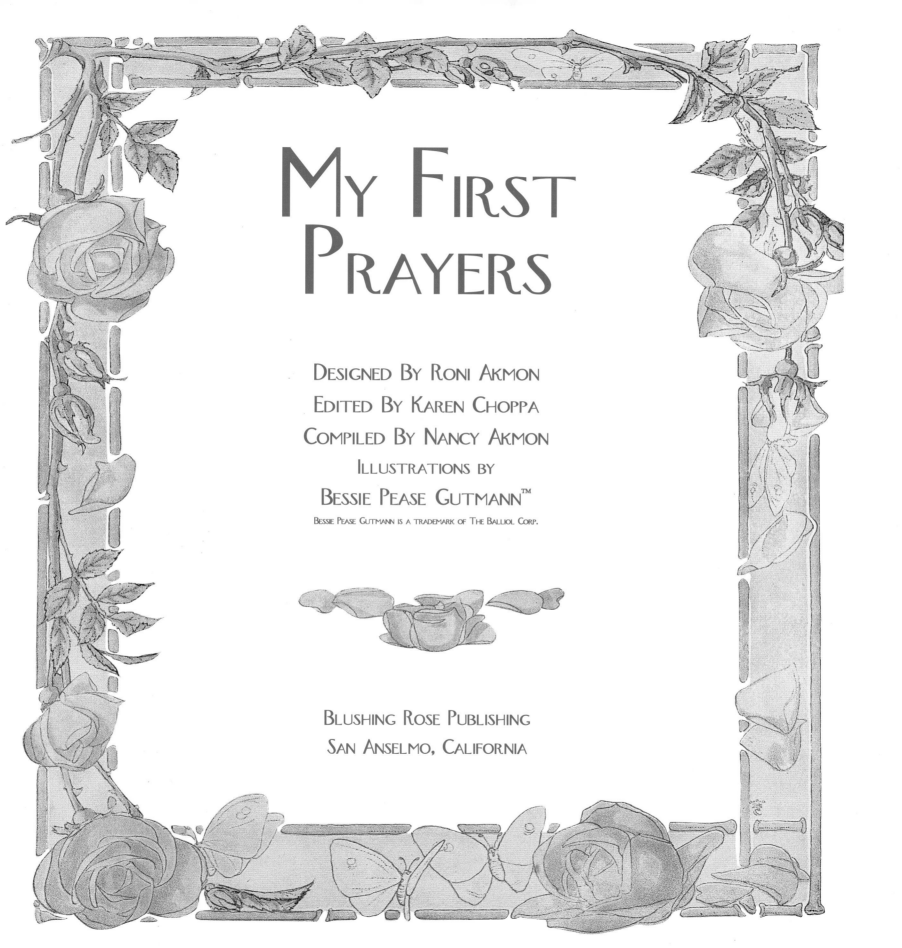

My First Prayers

Designed By Roni Akmon

Edited By Karen Choppa

Compiled By Nancy Akmon

Illustrations by

Bessie Pease Gutmann™

Bessie Pease Gutmann is a trademark of The Balliol Corp.

Blushing Rose Publishing

San Anselmo, California

For:

_____

With Love From:

_____

Date:

_____

Cover Illustration and interior illustrations by Bessie Pease Gutmann. These illustrations are reprinted with the permission of the Balliol Corporation. Designed by Roni Akmon. Text edited by Karen Choppa. Compiled by Nancy Akmon

ISBN# 1-884807-52-6

Blushing Rose Publishing
P.O. Box 2238
San Anselmo, Ca. 94979
www.blushingrose.com

Printed in China

Day by day,
dear Lord, of Thee
Three things I pray:
To see Thee more
clearly,
To love Thee more
dearly,
To follow Thee more
nearly, day by day.

St. Richard of Chichester

Matthew, Mark, Luke, and John,
Bless the bed that I lie on.
Four corners to my bed,
Four angels 'round my head,
One to watch and one to pray
And two to bear my soul away.

Traditional

DEAR FATHER, HEAR AND BLESS
THY BEASTS AND SINGING BIRDS,
AND GUARD WITH TENDERNESS
SMALL THINGS THAT HAVE NO WORDS.

UNKNOWN

I SEE THE MOON,

AND THE MOON SEES ME;

GOD BLESS THE MOON,

AND GOD BLESS ME.

UNKNOWN

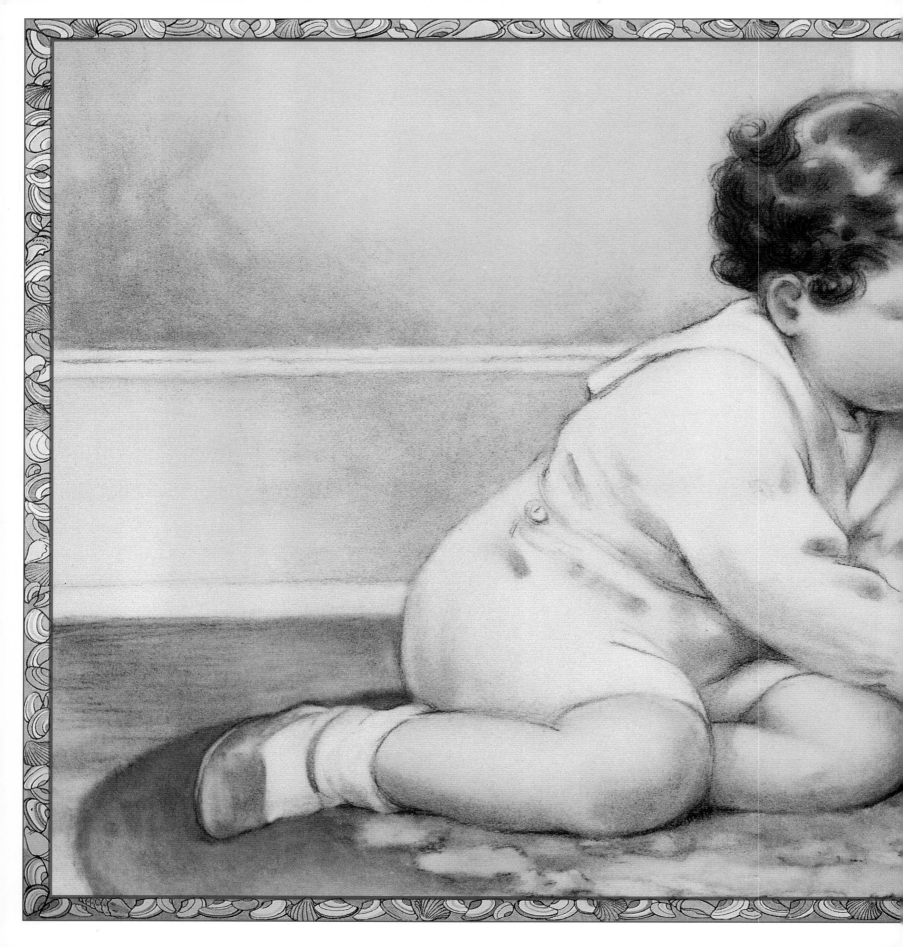

LORD MAKE MY LIFE A LITTLE LIGHT,
WITHIN THE WORLD TO GLOW;
A LITTLE FLAME THAT BURNS SO BRIGHT,
WHEREVER I MAY GO.

LORD MAKE MY LIFE A LITTLE HYMN
OF TENDERNESS AND PRAISE;
OF FAITH THAT NE'ER GROWS DIM,
TO ALL YOUR WONDROUS WAYS.

FROM A CHILD'S HYMN
BY M. BETHAM—EDWARDS

THOU ART GREAT
AND THOU ART
GOOD,
AND WE THANK THEE
FOR THIS FOOD.

TRADITIONAL

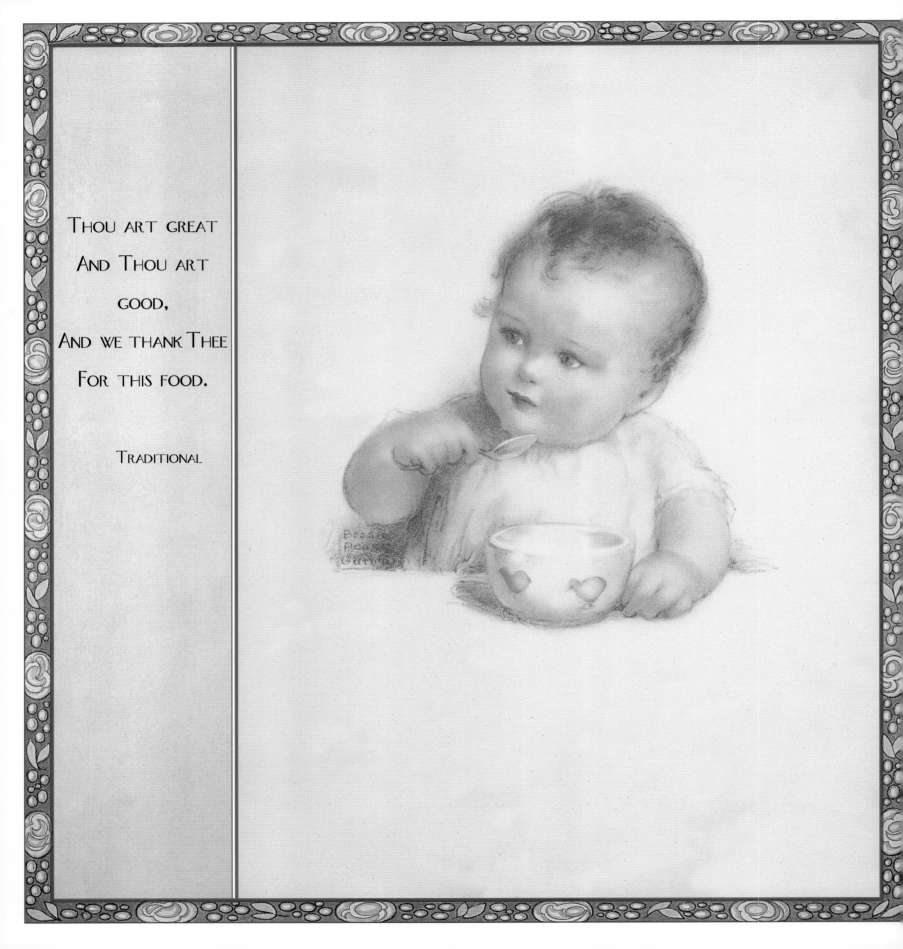

Now I lay me down
to sleep,
I pray Thee, Lord,
my soul to keep;
Thy love be with me
through the night
And wake me with
the morning light.

Traditional

FATHER, WE THANK
THEE FOR THE NIGHT,
AND FOR THE PLEASANT
MORNING LIGHT,
FOR REST AND FOOD
AND LOVING CARE,
AND ALL THAT MAKES
THE WORLD SO FAIR.

HELP US DO THE THINGS
WE SHOULD,
TO BE TO OTHERS KIND
AND GOOD,
IN ALL WE DO,
IN ALL WE SAY,
TO GROW MORE LOVING
EVERY DAY.

UNKNOWN

Our Father who art
in heaven,
Hallowed be Thy name.
Thy kingdom come,
Thy will be done,
On earth as
it is in heaven.
Give us this day
our daily bread,
And forgive us our
trespasses,
As we forgive those
who trespass
against us.
And lead us not into
temptation,
But deliver us
from evil,
For thine is the
kingdom,
And the power, and
the glory,
Forever and ever.
Amen.

Traditional

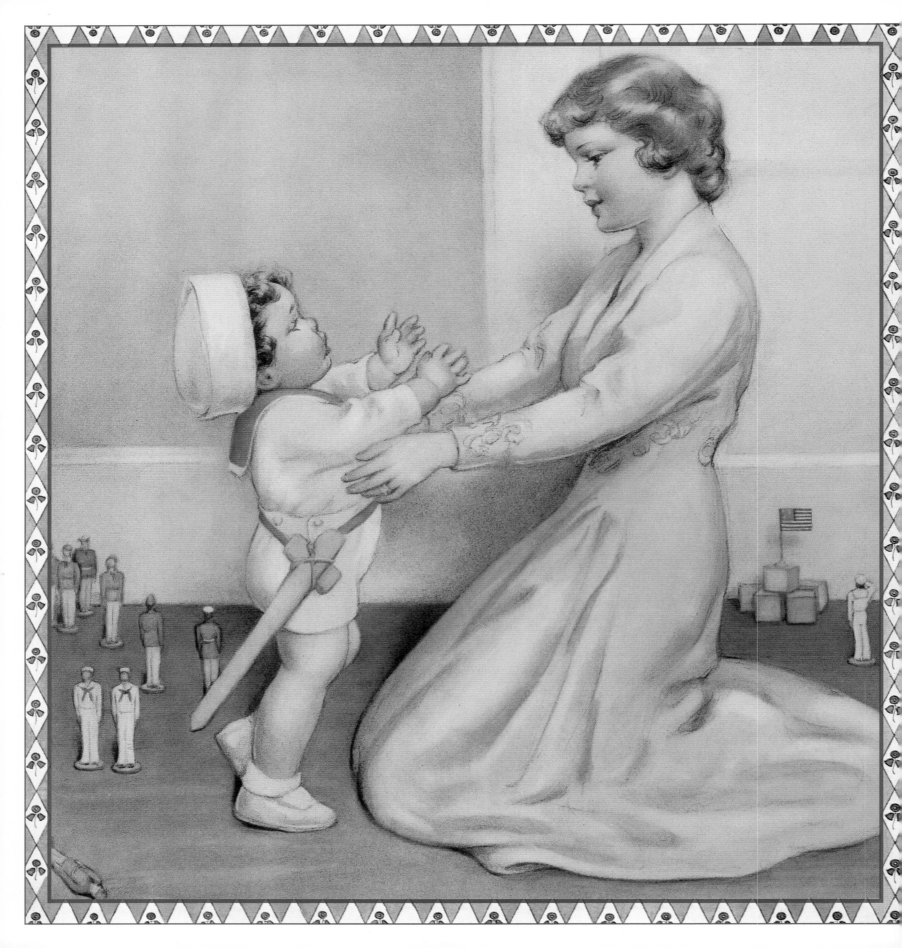

For the Lord is good;

His mercy is everlasting;

And His truth endureth

to all generations.

from Psalm 100

For mother-love and father-care,
For brothers strong and sisters fair,
For love at home and here each day,
For guidance lest we go astray,
Father in heaven, we thank Thee.

For this new morning with its light,
For rest and shelter of the night,
For health and food,
for love and friends,
For ev'rything His goodness sends,
Father in heaven, we thank Thee.

For flowers that bloom
about our feet,
For tender grass, so fresh, so sweet,
For song of bird and hum of bee,
For all things fair we hear and see,
Father in heaven, we thank Thee.

For blue of stream and blue of sky,
For pleasant shade of branches high,
For fragrant air and cooling breeze,
For beauty of the blooming trees,
Father in heaven, we thank Thee.

Unknown

ANGEL OF GOD,
MY GUARDIAN DEAR,
TO WHOM THE
LORD'S LOVE
ENTRUSTS ME HERE.
ALL THIS DAY
BE AT MY SIDE
TO LOVE AND GUARD,
TO HELP AND GUIDE.

UNKNOWN

I will praise Thee, O Lord,

with my whole heart;

I will show forth all thy

marvelous works.

I will be glad and rejoice in Thee:

I will sing praise to thy name,

O Thou most high.

From Psalm 9

All things bright and beautiful,
All creatures, great and small,
All things wise and wonderful,
The Lord God made them all.

He gave us eyes to see them,
And lips that we might tell
How great is God Almighty,
Who has made all things well!

from The Creation
by Cecil Frances Alexander

GOD MADE THE WORLD SO BROAD AND GRAND,

FILLED WITH BLESSINGS FROM HIS HAND.

HE MADE THE SKY SO HIGH AND BLUE,

AND ALL THE LITTLE CHILDREN, TOO.

UNKNOWN

We sleep that we may wake renewed,
To serve Thee as Thy children should,
With love and zeal and gratitude,
God of the weary.

from Evening Hymn
by M. Betham-Edwards

I thank you Lord,
At the end of day,
For the fun I've had
At work and play.
God, thank You too,
For a bed so warm
Where now I'll sleep
Safe from any harm.

By Karen Choppa

THE YEAR'S AT
THE SPRING,
AND DAY'S AT
THE MORN;
MORNING'S AT SEVEN;
THE HILLSIDE'S
DEW-PEARLED;
THE LARK'S ON
THE WING;
THE SNAIL'S ON
THE THORN:
GOD'S IN HIS HEAVEN-
ALL'S RIGHT WITH
THE WORLD!

PIPPA'S SONG

ROBERT BROWNING

O Lord, may I
never give
pain to things that
feel and live:
Let the gentle
robin come
For the crumbs I save
at home.
Let me ne'er hurt
the timid hare
Peeping from her
green grass lair,
I'll let her come and
hop and play
On the lawn at
close of day.
The little lark goes
soaring high
To the bright
windows of the sky,
Singing as if 'twere
always spring,
And fluttering on an
untired wing;
I'll let him sing his
happy song,
Nor do these gentle
creatures wrong.

Unknown

Be beside me
in the light,
Close by me through
all the night;
Make me gentle,
kind, and true,
Do what mother
bids me do;
Help and cheer me
when I fret,
And forgive me
when I forget.

from A Little Child's Hymn
—Francis Turner Palgrave

GOOD MORNING

NOW THE SUN
IS IN THE SKIES,
FROM MY BED
AGAIN I RISE;
LORD, THOU
NEVER—SETTING SUN,
SHINE ON ME,
THY LITTLE ONE.

LORD, ALMIGHTY
KING ABOVE,
THEE I PRAY FOR
THOSE I LOVE;
LORD, WHO LOVEST
MORE THAN I,
HELP THEM FROM THY
THRONE ON HIGH.

FROM MORNING HYMN

BY R.F. LITTLEDARE

KIND SHEPHERD, SEE,
THY LITTLE LAMB
COMES VERY TIRED
TO THEE;
O FOLD ME IN
THY LOVING ARMS,
AND SMILE ON ME.

I'VE WANDERED FROM
THY FOLD TODAY,
AND COULD NOT
HEAR THEE CALL;
AND O! I WAS NOT
HAPPY THEN,
NOR GLAD AT ALL.

I WANT, DEAR LORD,
TO BE SO GOOD,
AND FOLLOW CLOSE
TO THEE,
THROUGH SPRINGTIME
MEADOWS AND
PASTURES GREEN
AND ALWAYS HAPPY BE.

FROM THE GOOD SHEPHERD

BY H.P. HAWKINS

AND THOU SHALT
LOVE THE LORD THY
GOD WITH ALL
THINE HEART,
AND WITH ALL
THY SOUL,
AND WITH ALL
THY MIGHT.
AND THESE WORDS
I COMMAND YOU
TODAY SHALL BE
IN YOUR HEART.

DEUTERONOMY 6:5–6:6

THIS IS THE DAY
WHICH THE LORD
HAS MADE;
WE WILL REJOICE
AND BE GLAD.

FROM PSALM 118

THOUGH WE ARE
YOUNG AND SIMPLE,
IN PRAISE
WE MAY BE BOLD;
THE CHILDREN
IN THE TEMPLE
HE HEARD IN
DAYS OF OLD.
AND IF OUR HEARTS
ARE HUMBLE,
HE SAYS TO YOU
AND ME,
"SUFFER THE LITTLE
CHILDREN,
AND LET THEM COME
TO ME."

THEREFORE WE WILL
COME NEAR HIM,
AND SOLEMNLY
WE'LL SING;
NO CAUSE TO SHRINK
OR FEAR HIM,
WE'LL MAKE OUR
VOICES RING;
FOR IN OUR
TEMPLES SPEAKING,
HE SAYS TO
YOU AND ME.
"SUFFER THE LITTLE
CHILDREN,
AND LET THEM
COME TO ME."

BY E.P. HOOD

The Lord is my Shepherd;
I shall not want.
He maketh me to lie down in green pastures;
He leadeth me beside the still waters.
He restoreth my soul.

He leadeth me in the paths of righteousness
For His name's sake.
Yea, though I walk through the valley of the shadow of death,
I will fear no evil:
For Thou art with me;
Thy rod and thy staff
They comfort me.

Thou preparest a table before me
In the presence of mine enemies;
Thou anointest my head with oil;
My cup runneth over.
Surely goodness and mercy shall follow me
All the rest of my days:
And I will dwell in the house of the Lord
For ever.

Psalm 23

Do you know how many stars

There are shining in the skies?

Do you know how many clouds

Ev'ry day go floating by?

God in heaven has counted all,

He would miss one should it fall.

Do you know how many children

Go to little beds at night,

And without care or sorrow,

Wake up in the morning light?

God in heaven each name can tell,

Loves me, too, and loves me well.

From the German

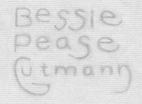

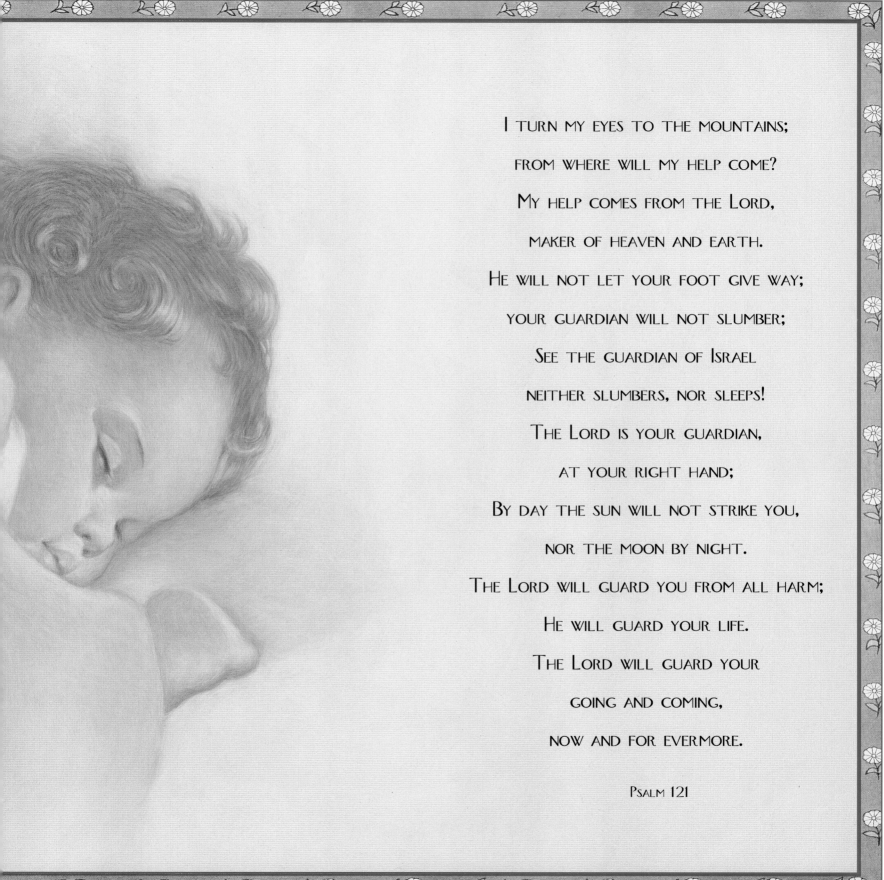

I TURN MY EYES TO THE MOUNTAINS;

FROM WHERE WILL MY HELP COME?

MY HELP COMES FROM THE LORD,

MAKER OF HEAVEN AND EARTH.

HE WILL NOT LET YOUR FOOT GIVE WAY;

YOUR GUARDIAN WILL NOT SLUMBER;

SEE THE GUARDIAN OF ISRAEL

NEITHER SLUMBERS, NOR SLEEPS!

THE LORD IS YOUR GUARDIAN,

AT YOUR RIGHT HAND;

BY DAY THE SUN WILL NOT STRIKE YOU,

NOR THE MOON BY NIGHT.

THE LORD WILL GUARD YOU FROM ALL HARM;

HE WILL GUARD YOUR LIFE.

THE LORD WILL GUARD YOUR

GOING AND COMING,

NOW AND FOR EVERMORE.

PSALM 121

THANK THEE, LORD, FOR MILK AND BREAD,

HOME AND TOYS AND BOOKS WE'VE READ,

AND MAKE ME LIKE TO GO TO BED.

FIVE O'CLOCK GRACE

BY CORA CASSARD TOOGOOD

"God is great; God is good."

This is the prayer we pray.

"We thank you for the food we eat;

"And for each brand new day.

"Thank you, God, for mom and dad.

"Thank you, God, for all we have.

"God is great; God is good."

This is the prayer we pray.

...Thank You God

by Karen Choppa

Bless my eyes
That I may see
Every flower,
Bird and bee.

Bless my nose
That I may sniff
Fresh baked cookies
Yum, chocolate chip!

Bless my ears
That I may hear
The ice cream truck
When it comes near.

Bless my lips
That I may say,
"Please" and "Thank you"
Every day.

Bless my hands
That I may hold
A new–born kitten
Just one week old.

Bless my legs
That I may run
And jump and dance
And have such fun.

Bless my mind
That I may learn
And then teach others
In return.

Bless my heart
That I may grow,
And love and kindness
Always show.

Bless every freckle,
Every hair;
Keep all of me
In Your tender care.
by Karen Choppa

THE

When the sun has left the hilltop,

And the daisy-fringe is furled,

When the birds from wood and meadow

In their hidden nests are curled,

Then I pray for all the children

That are sleeping in the world....

from *A Blessing for the Blessed*

by Laurence Alma Tadema

LOVE

Bessie
Pease
Gutmann

THANK THEE, FATHER, FOR THY CARE;

THOU ART WITH ME EVERYWHERE.

KEEP THY LITTLE CHILD, I PRAY,

HAPPY, GOOD AND TRUE TODAY.

MORNING PRAYER

BY CORA CASSARD TOOGOOD

LORD HELP ME
KNOW YOU
IN MY OWN HEART,
IN ALL I SAY
AND THINK AND DO;
LORD HELP ME
KNOW YOU
IN EVERY PART
OF THIS,
MY LIFE
I LIVE FOR YOU.

KAREN CHOPPA

THE LORD BIDS
US SHINE
WITH A PURE
CLEAR LIGHT,
LIKE A LITTLE CANDLE
BURNING IN THE NIGHT;
IN THE WORLD
IS DARKNESS,
SO WE MUST SHINE-
YOU IN YOUR
SMALL CORNER,
AND I IN MINE.

FROM THE LORD BIDS US SHINE

BY EMILY H. MILLER

For the lessons
I must learn,
Dear, Lord, bless
all who teach me;
Let them show me
right from wrong
Through their
actions,
I beseech Thee.

For Teachers
by Karen Choppa

Thank you, Lord,
for this day;
For my work and
for my play;
For my body and
for my soul,
Thank you, Lord,
who makes me whole.

Thank You, Lord

by Karen Choppa

FATHER IN HEAVEN
HEAR MY PRAYER;
KEEP ME IN
THY LOVING CARE
BE MY GUIDE
IN ALL I DO;
BLESS ALL THOSE
WHO LOVE ME TOO.

AMEN